SLEEP
NESS

Paul Hetherington

Paul Hetherington has created in SLEEPLESSNESS a travelogue of waking dreams, touring the meanders of the body and of the mind from three to six a.m. Well known for his prose poetry, in this collection he utilizes the page as a visual analogue for ruminations and sensations that arrive in waves, the slight stanzas moving delicately yet relentlessly down and across the page. In four sections, the poems travel far and wide, mapping the night as though it were one of Calvino's invisible cities. Rich in allusion (TALE OF GENJI, THE PILLOW BOOK, Bashō), spare yet lush in language, SLEEPLESSNESS entices the reader to risk traversing the dark in order to partake of its mysteries.

> **Holly Iglesias**
> Author of BOXING INSIDE THE BOX: WOMEN'S PROSE POETRY and SLEEPING THINGS

In Paul Hetherington's SLEEPLESSNESS, two lovers traverse a landscape—at once tangible and metaphoric—of insomnia, intimacy, desire, and language. In short lines tight with the tension of waiting, and stanzas like steps between sleep or the moments between touch, this book-length poem explores the 'wildness within our bodies.' Spanning cultures, eras, and mythologies, Hetherington's striking images crackle with electricity, offering shocks of recognition, the page tightening 'as if it's a sail.' We are passengers on this boat of dreams, adrift on the waves of his words, recognizing ourselves in the landscape, its powerful and arduous 'love of betweenness.'

> **Kristin Sanders**
> Author of THIS IS A MAP OF THEIR WATCHING ME, ORTHOREXIA and CUNTRY

Copyright © 2023 **Paul Hetherington**
All Rights Reserved

First Edition, First Printing — December 2023
Library of Congress Control Number: 2023944561
ISBN 978-1-953136-62-6   Hardback
ISBN 978-1-953136-61-9   Paperback
ISBN 978-1-953136-64-0   Audiobook

Cover Design by Kurt Lovelace
Cover Art by Pierian Springs Press
Cover type *Bauhaus Dessau* **Alfarn** by Céline Hurka,
Elia Preuss, Flavia Zimbardi,
Hidetaka Yamasaki, and Luca Pellegrini.
Poetry title and body set in **URW Baskerville**.
Misc. in **Jenson** by Robert Slimbach & **Sabon** by Jan Tschichold.
Flourishes set in Emigre Foundry **Dalliance,** by Frank Heine &
Emigre Foundry **ZeitGuys,** by Bob Aufuldish, Eric Donelan.
Typefaces licensed Adobe, Linotype, & URW GmbH.

PSPress.Pub
Pierian Springs Press, Inc
30 N Gould St, Ste 30
Sheridan, Wyoming 82801

'... O sleep, O gentle sleep,
  Nature's soft nurse, how have I frightened thee'

                  William Shakespeare
                  HENRY IV, PART 2

Contents

3 AM 1

4 AM 23

5 AM 53

6 AM 87

About the Author   109

Acknowledgments   111

Also by Paul Hetherington   112

Foreword

SLEEPLESSNESS is a postmodern pillow book charting desire's insomnolence. In a series of fissured fragments beginning at 3 a.m. 'with a wide bed as a harbour' and ending with a 6 a.m. aubade, the narrator writes back to Sei Shōnagon's THE PILLOW BOOK, politicising pleasure by revealing language's chimeric intimacies. This work sits beguilingly at the boundary between bodily knowledge and language's attempts to catch and name, transforming the idea of in-betweenness into a thrilling threshold between intimacy and strangeness, ardour and uncertainty, and speaking and silence. Where Shōnagon writes, 'At any time and in any place I find moonlight very moving,' the narrator's experience is 'a tense inveigling of opaque night.' Here, the susurration of the word *sleeplessness* belies its agony—the excruciations and ecstasies of insomnia are bound up in its very unspeakableness and ineffability.

Murasaki Shikibu's TALE OF GENJI (c.1000) and Matsuo Bashō's THE NARROW ROAD TO THE DEEP NORTH (first published posthumously in 1702) are also important intertextual references in SLEEPLESSNESS and provide shifting vocabularies and identities for the narrator. In SLEEPLESSNESS, the narrator's fascination with the author Murasaki Shikibu stems from his admiration for her as the world's first novelist, and also for her exploration of gender relations in the early eleventh century. The narrator responds to Murasaki's subversive use of language in a powerful moment of empathy where he inhabits the text: 'I say I live best / in Murasaki's words.'

Furthermore, for the narrator, 'Murasaki's verbs / are like secateurs'; they prune language, exposing its inadequacies even as it is written, which also connects to the severed lines that are such a distinctive feature of SLEEPLESSNESS. This form of poetry resonates with Japanese modes of verse, such as the haiku, haibun, zuihitsu and the prose poem, but it achieves its sense of vulnerability primarily from the fissures that break the lines apart into small pieces. Significantly, poems appear almost like bonsai trees, pruned and shaped into miniature branches that connect across the page.

In this way, SLEEPLESSNESS is invested in space and in the words unfurling down the page like a scroll being opened. In the spaces created between the words we see Hetherington's elegant use of Waldroppian gap gardening, where gaps are presented as moments of transformation that create various experiences of aporia.

SLEEPLESSNESS is deeply ecofeminist in its consideration of the politics of desire, writing after Shōnagon and Murasaki. The natural environment plays a key role in the liminal ruminations that keep the narrator awake, with some of the poems alluding to Bashō's travel diary written in haibun, THE NARROW ROAD TO THE DEEP NORTH. SLEEPLESSNESS responds in a series of repetitions and hauntings to the reading and recalling of Bashō's work until his name becomes an incantation or summoning of the poet and his poetry. These ruminations, in turn, also connect to both Shōnagon's and Murasaki's writing because of their suggestive, diary-like form and structure, and Hetherington prioritises these texts as powerfully political in their daily recordings of life.

In the narrator's sleep deprived mind, he sees 'one of Bashō's pink shells' before him. It is a remnant of nature, a metonym for the beach and its pleasures, and it also references the small transient cherry blossoms of Spring along with the memory of a lover. Bashō writes 'Behind this door / Now buried in deep grass, / A different generation will celebrate / The Festival of Dolls', and the narrator is beguiled by the environment he presents, so that the Mogami River winds like the helix of an earlobe:

> Words of Bashō
> decorate speaking
> with valleys and plants
>
> I climb in a pine tree
> and tread on moss
> under the skies
> above Mogami River
>
> Your earlobe beguiles me

In such ways, the sleepless night becomes a doorway into a state of becoming, generating a language that connotes a condition of perpetual and seductive inquiry, asking the reader to understand themselves newly.

SLEEPLESSNESS is also invested in the postmodern sublime. The four sets of interlocking sequences explore the difficulties of translating elusive experiences, largely of desire and the ineffable, into poetry. The fissuring and fracturing that results suggest the relics of a relationship connected to nature and, also, intimations of a wanderlust. Framed by invocations of Japanese history and contemporary culture—indeed, Japan is the world's most sleep deprived country—there is relief for the narrator in the rising sun, when dawn opens its doorway. Yet the poem remains as a lingering threshold that the narrator may or may not be able to cross into the new day. Although dawn temporarily ends the enduring night, the narrator 'cannot answer' the question, 'When will we sleep?'. All that lies ahead is 'the precipitous mountain' and the problematics associated with sleep.

Cassandra Atherton
Tokyo, Japan
November, 2023

SLEEP

NESS

Sleeplessness

with a wide bed as harbour

        Sleeplessness

        and tonight's bleaching vista

                A taste, a shape,
                a town's pale square—

                triangle and spire,

                a tense inveigling
                of opaque night

Syllables

balking at language

                    Syllables

                    that language pursues

                                        A breathed syllable
                                        crossing an earlobe—

                                        a furred caterpillar
                                        traversing a burrow

The clockface and 'now',

etched minutes and acid hours,

this sleeplessness

        The clockface and 'now'

        arriving snapshots
        and rotating ideas,

        acid hours

                The clockface fractured

                by wordy incisions
                and chiselling loss,

                acid hours and sleeplessness

Your body's here,
pressing down,

a failed analogy

a heavy suitcase

                    Your body's here

                    as pressing idea
                    on blue, watched squares
                    with the clutch

                    of what-is-desired

                                      Your toes follow
                                      a cathedral's long staircase

The body stretched,

an impossible archway,

another's muscle

                    Wine and slow words
                    washing a clockface,

                    tonguings of feeling

                                      Lip and thigh

                                      as abstractions,

                                      language's sketchy
                                      denotations

A high, flecked window

light as a creek
carousing on boulders

                A poised second-hand,

                an incipience speaking
                with mime's

                emphasis

                                The spoken
                                as spear,

                                that word, 'love'

                                and its question mark

The spoken steepening
on stony slopes

'Can we?' 'Are we?'

        The minotaur's labyrinth
        as analogy for feeling,

        blood-reaches of stars

                Speaking taken
                into a gaping mouth

                against ideas

                of what can't be done

To climb and fall
in a single motion,

turbulent hands
gripping the climber

                    A stooping eternity
                    of 'now' and 'is'

                                      Caramel knows
                                      your body's salt

                                      an evaporation
                                      or *fleur de sel*,

                                      tongues finding
                                      crevices

'Touch my arms'

  Pleasure ignites
  three a.m. absence

  in a species of anguish

        'Let's shift beds'

        'Look at that clockface
         blinking in purple
         like a raddled man'

              A minotaur's bellow,

              blood on the lip

A mouthful of coffee
as adored bitterness,

which your words keep sipping

                    Breathed syllables
                    in an extended reach—

                    green-and-white distance

                    a shoreline and city

                                      Breathed syllables
                                        and a bowl of fruit,

                                        rapid fruit flies

Your sentences
are a body's taut sinews

                Deluged feelings return
                to oceans of travel

                                Possession is

                                a boat bumping on water

This weight of dropped years,

a jetty, a diver

                      Sleeplessness

                      amid throes of languor

                                          The air's hands jostle,

                                          windows stare
                                          at an ankle-length dress

'You', 'I',
  a mess of pronouns

            We shop and walk,
            wanting a bedroom

                        Syllables drop

                        Bending, you search
                        but do not retrieve them

My arm on your waist,

your eyes travelling
parsecs of distance

                The cathedral congests
                with gargoyle belief

                as you reject
                adhesive surveillance

                                A word roams
                                like a cat in a garden

                                to purr at our feet

Lip and archway,

lip and arrow,

a kissing bow,

a fletched, wide mouth

        We turn and you brush
        my upper thigh,

        a calligrapher's letter

                This night would dream
                of a brazen room

                and the etching light
                of an ancient cup

We keep to shadows

We follow paths
to paintings by Goya

                You have me in hand,
                your words make a circle

                                The white days between us,

                                  the clock's slow sandhills

Dreams where I meet you,

a second-hand's chiding

                    Now you traverse
                    language's floodland

                                      Light shatters the blind
                                      that carries your image

Syllables lie
like discarded clothes

The inarticulate body
refusing language —

an incipience,

yet

almost
spoken

        A cry

        meaning 'savanna',
      'forest',
      'windblown tundra',

       a dug shout

       this conflagration

Black ground,
saturations of meadow and wildflower,

down-reaches of gullies,

lemon and purple
detonations

                      Clambering thought
                      to cross the divide,

                      crampons pressed

Sight tensing
and a siphoning landscape

        Smears of sunshine

        and eclipse's circumference —

        dark spears
        of shadowed
        feeling

Lull,

wide waterways

                      Waveforms

                      making caress out of stone

The body
as insinuating notion

as breath climbs thermals,

as language bathes
in the cerulean

                        In the sun's glare,
                        nudging connections —

                        brushed gestures,
                        fugitive beakings

Hands among wind

that's like a tightening apron—

Fly-away petals

becoming a lesson
in spiral geometry

Circumstance purrs—

rock face,
sun glance,
bodies becoming
a self-enclosed circle

        You say 'I don't know this',

        which is a body's
        intimate strangeness

Sun slide, blooms,
a waterfall,

weighted footsteps,

words tipping
to syllabic candour

                          A blackbird casting
                          its sheet-metal sound,
                          as if to proclaim
                          the end of speaking,

                          the bird's beak
                          stuttering on soil

Wildness crying
within our bodies

(like the obdurate blackbird,
or as animals cry)

sunscape,

scrabble,

a canyon of leaves

                                        Finding horizons
                                        in the near mind,

                                        searching latitudes

Wings scooping air,

a layer of down

                              The body hunching
                              into an arrow's flight

                              to earth,
                              droplets,
                              bogland,
                              sedge

Rain
as murmur

washing the throat

                        The bird's flight entangled
                        in wordy congestion,

                        a chased creature
                        among tendrils and boughs,

                        twining mythology

Orphic mysteries
dress your body
in light's golden fleece,

stones are charmed
by waveforms' caress

                    We're made from mysteries,

                    blood-knowledge sipping
                    memory's water

You enter again
the relinquished cerulean,

rising quickly
through blue and purple

                                        Your body becomes
                                        a simple archway,

                                        categories collapse

Returning,

your name
is a divination,

your body becomes
Hecate practising
her love of betweenness

                        Returning, we find
                        the walls and city
                        and stony slopes,

                        sketching tiles
                        with pressing endearments

On an old vase
a Minoan bull

tosses a woman

                              In this hallway
                              brown, straddling light

                              examines kisses

Behind the sofa
the carpet recollects

thrown-over midnight

                              A body, a tree,

                                  a rescued rosebud

'The music,' you say,
'is like our anthem'—
 electric guitar
 and gravelly voice,

a lyre in your hand

                            We are sleepless among
                            memory's debris

Words return
and we say a poem
through to the climax

                    Your legs are a phrase
                    it takes minutes to utter

Our beginnings belong
in our repetitions

                    You say, 'Don't forget.'

                    I say, 'Please remember.'

You and I
exchange our pronouns

                                    Your arm on my waist,
                                    my eyes gazing inwards

The words we say,
like a painting by Monet—

those punctuations
of kissing color

                        Your feathered body
                        cresting sheets

                        that also wrap you

A hesitation,
like a calligrapher's brush
poised above

a first

horizontal

                                  Writing pleasure

                                  with a similar gesture

The delicate Washi,
this written-on skin

                              The bird as brush,

                              letter as inscape

The bird as a feather

fletching desire

            Your repeating question:
            how do we write this?

Your repeating request:
write it again

                    A word stands
                    like a bird in a bath

                    sipping and singing

The calligrapher's brush
summons horizons

                We press again
                to the vertical strokes

Clouding feeling,

a view to a mountain
scaled by language—

rain and fog,
a veil's image

                Migrating across
                mountain slopes—
                snow,

                a dream
                of being emperor

                                A descent as slippery
                                as soap on a rockface

                                (the body slides
                                in the filling bath),

                                light that glosses
                                a ridge's shoulder

Words
darkening
above the snowline,

a neckline framing recollection

                The spa bath coughs
                exclamations
                onto a knee,

                a mountain declivity,
                rivulets

                        Tense boughs
                        and a girding of remnant blossom,

                        a body behind

                        cloudy glass

Reading Bashō,

minutes that idle
with twenty scenes

        Reading Bashō,

        and your robe falls
        in an unforeseen flurry

                Reading Bashō.

                Your toes curl
                like okinami

Decisive touch
and hesitancy,

a prickling of pine needles

                  Staccato talk,

                  the cracking of ice

                                    The filled glass
                                    refracting memory,

                                    bubbles too rapid
                                    to expand into speech

Your words, 'I'm waiting',

a teetering ice platform,

a wind-flustered slope

                Your words
                are red fire

                in evening's cave

                              Your reading becomes
                              a climb to a lookout

                              and plummeting

                              sight

I revere
a notion of your body

You ask how to dress
to make it real

                        The real overwrites
                        long-hauled notions

                                        Snow-whiteness as somewhere
                                        you don't inhabit,

                                        an escalation
                                        of flushed ideas

I follow your spine
like thirty-three steps

The revered temple
is nearly in view

           ' Love me,' you say,

               meaning something else

                             You read aloud
                             another poem—

                             identical words,

                             different inflections

We're absorbed in the view—

words like roads
and stretching provinces

Arashiyama's bamboo forest

        Our upright feelings,

        long breaches of green

                We're disturbed by touch—

                as a passing ski churns
                water it skims

Now we find words
crossing a folio
like distant pilgrims
out of a cave—

marking the snow
with steady footsteps,

their colorful cloaks
a swirl of brushstrokes

                    You follow their gestures
                    with a pointing finger

                    The tracing of touch
                    becomes a drawn line

                                    A forest location,

                                    a shadowed reach,
                                    as if long boughs
                                    push into feeling—

                                    the forgetfulness
                                    new places occasion,

                                    reinscribing
                                    the looping pathways

A recollection
new places prompt,

touch hauling old feeling

as water is pulled
from a long-buried well

        Your finger follows
        a page's words

        One by one,
        step by step,

        it crosses terrain
        no-one has marked—

        this passage of skin

                We're deep in a glade,
                or is it a room

                We hear the sough
                of wind from slopes
                climbing above us

                Room and wilderness,
                old love and new

Cresting words,

a commotion like water
sliding on boulders

                You say we're safe
                in the paper-thin room,

                we look toward
                a hemline of snow
                dressing the mountain's

                uncanniness

                                    As if the earth

                                    knows desire's ruptures

Your body's cold
from swimming across
the frothing river

Your body's burning
from exertion

                    Travelling inwards
                    we encounter warmth—

                    an idea's solace,
                    a room's caught sunshine
                    like glossy paint,

                    and the body's junctures

                                      You're yellow with sun
                                      like Monet's lilies,

                                      flushed with effort
                                      like his path of roses

Words drop petals,

imbrication shedding
its lapping meanings

                        Words of Bashō
                        decorate speaking
                        with valleys and plants

                        I climb in a pine tree
                        and tread on moss
                        under the skies
                        above Mogami River

                        Your earlobe beguiles me

                                                 Your earlobe beguiles,

                                                 cranes congregate
                                                 on Shiogoshi beach,

                                                 I'm entranced
                                                 by your gait

Silence

as thought stills your hand
on the tickled page —

we have come to a moment
when gesture is beckoned

by otherness

        An uncodified
        language of rain —

        but what do I know
        of eloquence

        without full translation?

                Fingers as droplets
                that wind releases

                from overhead leaves

                Fingers as rainstorm

Rain courses through me
as trickles and runnels —

emotion splashed

through the rising body

        An escapade
        of stretching minutes —

        you speak of seasons

        Small scatters of mizzle

                Small scatters of mizzle

                spotting night's path
                among ancient light —

                a star pushing forth
                a lost century

You say this is new—
in the way of finding
what others have known
for thousands of years,

but was strange to your body

                Feeling emerges
                in thousands of shapes,

                spawnings of touch
                to crowd our thought
                with fly-away purples

                                We're pale ground
                                for the riotous pigment
                                of the dabbing brush

                                Slowly it builds
                                like a fantastical scene—

                                through astonishment
                                a waterfall

                                drops

A pointed pine needle
tickling an arm
as you turn from blossoms
assailing the path—

open, wet pinks

that corral observation

                A garden expands
                across bird-skimming water

                A single crane
                brings into focus
                a boulder it crosses,

                a blinking eye

                              Now you're the garden,

                              tying perspective
                              to the close-staring gaze

                              touch implies

A garden as room
overlooking a city—

touch's tendrils
entwining and branching

                    Below us, long trains
                    move toward distance

                    like an utterance
                    we're unable to read

                                      High in the air
                                      a clocktower shows
                                      midnight approaching

                                      Someone walks
                                    through a starless valley

You speak through bubbles
of fine champagne,

kisses of words
to make the mouth golden

                      You carry in hands
                      the tempestuous winter,

                      a damp, rosy cheek

                                          The hem of your skirt,
                                          the length of your coat

                                          We turn from the mall
                                          to find a taste

                                          of snow in our mouths

The city's kiss
that we take to our room

The length of your coat
and hem of your skirt

A form of obeisance

        Our legs in the bath,

        saplings that stand
        in a garden's still lake,

        your sudden stooping
        in testing the water

                Snow's recollection
                chasing your lips
                in the champagne

                you pull from the freezer

That taste of the mountain
when snow
and sunshine

rub together

                In the bath
                a passage swims
                like a bottlenose dolphin

                Your book is splashed
                by our exclamations

                                  We see the river
                                that Hokusai sketched
                                pressed by buildings

                                Where are the palimpsests
                                of lost centuries?

In the width of your robe
at the glimmering window,
you might be flying

The inexplicable city
has an animal's eyes

        Greens and reds
        are stroking your face

                Light blooms
                through insomniac night;
                at five-thirty a.m.

                Bashō sees the flowering reeds

Did someone leave here
one of Bashō's pink shells

from the Colored Beach?

                        Is there snow on your eyelid?

                        You bend toward me
                        to let me inspect it

                                              Is there snow on your eyelid?

                                              Your blinking eyes
                                              crinkle with laughter

You say your feelings
are hurrying

like the Express
to Takadanobaba

                    The station's music
                    conjures childhood

                    'All these years later,
                    how can a cartoon
                    provoke my tears?'

                                        You fasten your boots,

                                        talking of travellers
                                        in Hokusai's view
                                        of the back of Mt Fuji
                                        and Minobu River,

                                        the foaming of cloud

'I feel like his traveller
 balancing parcels'

             You unbutton your coat
             as we enter a mall

             The city's a creature
             flexing its back

                              Small shudders,

                              a clasping

Snow on the foothills
flung by wind,
like our tossed coverlet

You say, 'Feel my goosebumps'

        We share dark colors
        and jags of expression—

        like Hokusai's storm
        beneath the summit

                The spa bath froths
                like the aftermath

                of an okinami

                on a broken

                shoreline

A lathered body
clouding glass

with flying soapsuds

        Reading Bashō

        right to the end,

        considering
        adhesive clam-shells

                Reading Bashō

                as his words decorate
                your tightly tied robe

Cracking ice
as you push a bottle
into the bucket.

Long, empty glasses
and aimless hands

        Your words, 'I'm waiting',

        like a breeze
        that will soon
        fluster your robe

                Slant kinds of feeling,

                as the body begins
                to shake off language—

                a blossom skewing

                on scintillant water

After the mountains

travellers thaw
in the Kuroshio current

                A descent like diving

                into a lagoon
                of purple seaweed

                                Feelings pulse
                                like a moon jellyfish

                                in neon blue water

A room
and an ocean,

a bed
and raft,

a view of a mountain

                                    Lathering snow

                              A book is a door
                              slanting at morning,

                              words a membrane
                              misted by sun

                   The room disperses
                   night's revenants

Holding the book,
you roll in the sheets
as if with a lover

　　　　　　　　　Holding the book
　　　　　　　　　as if it's a body
　　　　　　　　　and, absurdly,

　　　　　　　　　trying to kiss

　　　　　　A body and book
　　　　　　as if each is the other—

　　　　　　as if words become blood

You sniff at pages
that nudge your pillow,

press endpapers
against your palm

>   Trying to find
>   yourself in translation

>   Like a new form of sleep,
>   or restlessness,
>
>   you start reading again

Eloquence
standing clear and apart,

like a Japanese castle

A language built
for long habitation

Murasaki's
indelible accents

like a vast architecture

or glistering lake

or ornate folding screen

Her words become water

with fumbling currents
throwing figures
onto the sibilant page

                    Words bubble toward
                    a 'dark purple dress'

          There are slivers of sunshine

          and quick skews of rain

As if your speech
wets the clean pages

                    Yet your voice
                    keeps the rhythm
                    of formal address

        It creates gardens
        already lost

        in the eleventh century

Words assume
the steps of a dance,

the sound of drumming

Despite formality

insouciance gathers
our arms and legs

Your reading addresses

vernacular feeling

Your mouth comprehends

banished views
of noble houses

The present swells

in excavations
of speaking's art

In its intricate bones
and elaborate grammar
your arm on the sheet

is like a time-worn sentence

There's manicured landscapes

we barely credit

At Middle River

rain falls inward

Hints of bodies
behind a screen

How to decipher
their unknown names?

You say words might be

a river crossing

                    Your running words

                    become perfumed liquid

          Language carries
          in its saturations

          our identities
          like a form of flotsam

How we float
away from each other

in language's lattice

                    Boats on a harbour,
                    expanses of water
                    which meanings

                    won't touch

          With a gale's onset
          the page starts to tighten

          as if it's a sail

We arrive at a shoreline,
inspecting shells
that the story ejects,

or they might be
our numerous failings.

                Near an old house

                we wander through
                shinobu grass

        An expedition
        into collaring desire

You speak of belonging
to viny language

more than to life

Then say, life is language,
entwining and tight—

'there's no separation'

Murasaki's verbs
are like secateurs

'I suppose literature
does stand apart.'

I say I live best
in Murasaki's words

　　　　　　　　'I'd hold you now
　　　　　　　　　behind a shoji screen'

　　　　Love's punctuations
　　　　cause your words

　　　　to dilate and halt

You read again

and it's as if the page
hangs a wide mirror

                    The language locates

                    spoiling thoughts
                    we refuse to name

       We circle ideas

       as Genji
       orbits Fujitsubo

This renewed flow of speaking
has the suck of a tide

                              Nouns we've gathered,
                              shells you pocketed,

                         sidelong meanings

         Love's a notion
         we'd now slide across

         a sense of unease

But your whisper is like
Dhaka muslin

                    As if to say,

                'When you can't sleep
                 I'll read it again'

        'How lovely' cried Genji
        'are those distances

        half lost in haze'

You close the book,
open the blind,

recoil from daylight

                We look at each other,

                disbelieving
                the absence of words

        Your hair flames
        as if you've stolen

        some sort of halo

'When will we sleep?'

  I cannot answer

Long slopes of stone,
a distant temple,

the precipitous mountain

Paul Hetherington

Paul Hetherington is a distinguished poet and Professor Emeritus at the University of Canberra, Australia. Among his 45 creative and critical books and chapbooks, and numerous scholarly chapters and articles, he has previously published 17 full-length collections of poetry, including **RAGGED DISCLOSURES** (RWP, 2022) and **HER ONE HUNDRED AND SEVEN WORDS** (MadHat Press, 2021).

His poetry has appeared in more than 70 anthologies and has won or been nominated for over 40 national and international awards and competitions, including **Pushcart Prize** nominations, and he recently won the **2021 Bruce Dawe National Poetry Prize**.

He is co-founding editor of the international online journal *AXON: CREATIVE EXPLORATIONS*, and he founded **International Poetry Studies** in the **Centre for Creative and Cultural Research** at his university in 2013. He founded the international **Prose Poetry Project** in 2014.

Paul also worked in the cultural sector, most notably for the **National Library of Australia**, where he was *Director of Publications and Events* for many years and founding editor of the influential quarterly humanities and literary journal *VOICES* (1991–97). Paul chaired the **ACT Cultural Council** (2005–13) and the **ACT Public Art Panel** (2006–11) and in these roles instigated various arts initiatives, including the development and delivery of the first comprehensive policy and action framework for public art in the **Australian Capital Territory**.

With Professor Cassandra Atherton he co-authored the authoritative 344-page **PROSE POETRY: AN INTRODUCTION** (Princeton University Press, 2020) and co-edited the definitive **ANTHOLOGY OF AUSTRALIAN PROSE POETRY** (Melbourne University Press, 2020).

Acknowledgments

From time to time, SLEEPLESSNESS alludes to, and once or twice quotes from the following books: Bashō, THE NARROW ROAD TO THE DEEP NORTH AND OTHER TRAVEL SKETCHES, translated by Nobuyuki Yuasa (Harmondsworth: Penguin, 1970); and Murasaki, THE TALE OF GENJI, translated by Arthur Waley (Boston: Houghton Mifflin, 1925). It also alludes more broadly to Sei Shōnagon's THE PILLOW BOOK.

An excerpt from SLEEPLESSNESS was published in *New American Writing*, no. 41, edited by Paul Hoover. Thanks to Cassandra Atherton for her wonderfully mercurial, creative and sometimes whimsical contributions to the genesis of this poem, and also for her marvellous editorial work. Thanks to Michelle Hetherington for her continuing and abiding inspiration and support. Thanks to Kurt Lovelace and **Pierian Springs Press** for their expertise and exemplary commitment to this work.

Also by Paul Hetherington

Fiction

BLOOD AND OLD BELIEF: A VERSE NOVEL
Canberra, ANU: Pandanus Books, 2003

Poetry Chapbooks

Sour
in FIVE TASTES
(with **Cassandra Atherton,
Oz Hardwick, Paul Munden, Jen Webb**)
Canberra: Recent Work Press, 2022, 53-77

The Golden Age
in FIVE AGES
(with **Cassandra Atherton, Oz Hardwick,
Paul Munden, Jen Webb**)
Canberra: Recent Work Press, 2021, 5-25

The Novel Reader
in C19: INTERTEXT || EKPHRASIS
(with **Cassandra Atherton, Paul Munden, Jen Webb**)
Canberra: Recent Work Press, 2020, 27-50

Smell
in THE SIX SENSES
(with **Cassandra Atherton, Paul Munden,
Jen Webb** and **Jordan Williams**)
Canberra: Recent Work Press, 2019, 27-50

WEDDING DRESS AND OTHER POEMS
Southern-Land Poets, Spring 2018,
Magill, SA: Garron Publishing, 2018

Audiobooks

SLEEPLESSNESS
Sheridan, WY: Pierian Springs Press, 2023

Poetry Chapbooks

PROSODY: ENJAMBMENT
Canberra: Authorised Theft, 2018

COLOURS: BLUE
Canberra: Authorized Theft, 2017

THE TAOIST ELEMENTS: EARTH
Canberra: Authorised Theft, 2016

JARS
Canberra: Authorised Theft, 2015

VISCERA: POEMS
(part of an exhibition with **Jen Webb**)
Canberra: Dancing Scorpion Press, 2014

SPECTRAL RESEMBLANCES
(with digital artist **Anita Fitton**)
Fairfield, Vic: Michael Silver, 2013

CHICKEN AND OTHER POEMS
Ed. **Judy Johnson**, *Wagtail* 119,
Newcastle: Picaro Press, April 2012

MAPPING WILDWOOD ROAD
Pamphlet Poets, Series One, No. 4
Canberra: National Library of Australia, 1990

Poetry

SLEEPLESSNESS
Sheridan, WY: Pierian Springs Press, 2023

RAGGED DISCLOSURES
Canberra: Recent Work Press, 2022

HER ONE HUNDRED AND SEVEN WORDS
Cheshire, MA: MadHat Press, 2021

FUGITIVE LETTERS
(with **Cassandra Atherton**)
Canberra: Recent Work Press, 2020

TYPEWRITER AND MANUSCRIPT
Melbourne, Vic: Life Before Man, 2020

PALACE OF MEMORY: AN ELEGY
Canberra: Recent Work Press, 2019

MOONLIGHT ON OLEANDER
Crawley, WA: UWA Publishing, 2018

ÍKAROS
Canberra: Recent Work Press, 2017

GALLERY OF ANTIQUE ART
Canberra: Recent Work Press, 2016

BURNT UMBER
Crawley, WA: UWA Publishing, 2016

WATCHING THE WORLD: IMPRESSIONS OF CANBERRA
(with photography by **Jen Webb**)
Canberra: Blemish Books, 2015

SIX DIFFERENT WINDOWS
Crawley, WA: UWA Publishing, 2013

Poetry

IT FEELS LIKE DISBELIEF
Cambridge, UK: Salt Publishing, 2007

STEPPING AWAY: SELECTED POEMS
Canberra: Molonglo Press, 2001

CANVAS LIGHT
Molonglo Press, 1998

SHADOW SWIMMER
Canberra: Molonglo Press, 1995

THE DANCING SCORPION
Canberra: Molonglo Press, 1993

ACTS THEMSELVES TRIVIAL
Fremantle: Fremantle Arts Centre Press, 1991

Artist's Books

Moon
(with **Cassandra Atherton** and **Phil Day**)
A concertina artist's book
Richmond, Vic: Mountains Brown Press, 2017

Dilly Dally
(with **Cassandra Atherton** and **Phil Day**)
A concertina artist's book
Richmond, Vic: Mountains Brown Press, 2016

www.ingramcontent.com/pod-product-compliance
Lightning Source LLC
Chambersburg PA
CBHW020444090526
44586CB00045B/852